only half-breathed air

a book of purasu ni

J.F. Merifield

Finishing Line Press
Georgetown, Kentucky

only half-breathed air

Copyright © 2025 by J.F. Merifield
ISBN 979-8-89990-279-6 First Edition
All rights reserved under International and Pan-American Copyright Conventions. No part of this book may be reproduced in any manner whatsoever without written permission from the publisher, except in the case of brief quotations embodied in critical articles and reviews.

Publisher: Leah Huete de Maines
Editor: Christen Kincaid
Cover Art: J.F. Merifield Photographer
Cover Design: Elizabeth Maines McCleavy

Order online: www.finishinglinepress.com
also available on amazon.com

Author inquiries and mail orders:
Finishing Line Press
PO Box 1626
Georgetown, Kentucky 40324
USA

—

in a mirror in a hall

the distance doubles

and, with truth, the air wavers

an unremarkable day

absolute, it ticks

by, collecting dust, not shine

salmonella everywhere

this boat, the drowning

and the spread of mold and rot

and from here we see the house

vacant and moth-balled

this dust is the sun, no breath

ate life without seasoning

how does one get here?

this sleep? this mess obnoxious

here unknown catastrophes

culminate in song

tragedies pool and flare up

what is this bridge that connects

i can tell of late

the panel vibrates, now loose

holding a memorial

for my memories

lost, forgotten, never had

there were songs fit to be us

and what wears within

siphon the glances for keeps

she pulls rips and flips her hair

drops star cluster stares

every second spills over

fingers could drum a rhythm

a spinal heartbeat

whispers trigger electric

could set the flood down upon

me; feathered, you fly

above, tight circles, dove-sight

you appear distant and nude

a lingering warmth

almost knowable, then gone

whenever i imagine

i know what you think

i am quickly proven wrong

if only i were the cave

you stole away in

curled away from the world, hid

that would have been our song on

the air waves, should have

been us dancing through the haze

what's left to say, a heart carved

up on the table

old scars cut again, again

ardor less than a trickle

a decades long drought

dust deep in desolation

no abilities i have

in reality

bring this dream into being

i can hope that one day soon

we will meet again

arms outstretched, a wrapped embrace

it is always gonna be

brutal, these hollows,

these depictions, observed grief

the next tattoo is asleep

raw space between clouds

a filling cemetery

we slow the circle's current

and the pause builds up

grows stronger with denial

just watch the rivers' trickle

down, flow divergence

this site is a hammer thrown

roadside apiaries swarm

with gusts and headrush

undone in the spray, the drag

kites catch the smell of death, swirl

with sea air empty

another end with buzz, fog

jaw unhinged, festering pus,

a ravenous burn,

wolf in the pulpit feasting

the glue horse still pulls the plow,

still burdened by greed,

reflection draws still again

still waiting for the mighty

waters to roll down

'cause fear is a wicked tool

our own choices got us here

the consequences

these results of complacence

so many traditions rule

so few are good, thus

cause and alarm ripple out

i no longer hear the word

that drew the world whole

mouthed, still i know its blossom

in the face of the world's wind

my eyes produce sand

results of this gravity

ten minutes in the mirror

how does your face feel?

raskolnikov and fatigued

to stay is to wait to die

sitting, pacing, here

in a room fleeced once again

please cease all marketing spam

this data product

knows it's human, not for sale

time for ash covering heads

faces rent like cloth

wails from more than just mothers

only a high cloud scathing

sky roils grey haze mist

a simmer ripple season

start the grieving in the space

between gravities

a maze in motions floats forth

the pace of the sun setting

leaves dusk covering

me, only dust motes adrift

i've got no wisdom for you

only half-breathed air

a collapse of tangled thought

be a draft, like a mule wind

a sweet bush skirted

both eyes settle the hillside

the moon will be located

in a different

place than where you last saw it

the experience of time—

a second here nor

there, an unseen passing by

hope just a second away

a shoreline of sand

a wave of realities

in the notes where sight was born

gathered a nest-storm

an awareness of not i

nourish rather than inflict

tough to hear and do

a swallowed measure of grace

For G.K. & C.M.

summer with painted flowers

summer with campfire

summer lead by servant strength

hands-on-hope is the real call

life-service not lip

grit sell to the convenient

notes of dry pine and sage grass

a mountain breeze blush

share the path with dung and dirt

leaf, branch, proof of breeze, a tree

rooted in the woods

surrounded by the earth's breath

For M.T.

on the dock reading the book

you recommended

autumn gold drifts in gentle

what language or word, symbol,

identifier,

signals water to birds' brains

a mountain lion perches

in a pine to pounce

silence present, wind hushes

sassafras tea on the stove

steaming in a pot

outdoors evening glows in depth

breathe deep, heavens hover near,

at night, stand outside

in the shadow of the earth

the milky way is a trench

dug and body-full

let the glow burn bright and blaze

Note:

The form, purasu ni (translates from Japanese as plus two), is an ode to, the haiku, tanka, senryu, renga forms. Purasu ni are the addition of two more syllables to the standard English haiku, 19 instead of 17, and are presented in 7-5-7 tercets. Purasu ni do not necessarily have to have a kireji, and similarly do not need to refer to the season. They can use punctuation, but do not have to. When presented as a collection, the total number of purasu ni should be in multiples of 19 (19, 38, 57, 76, ...). Image heavy, with nature a steady presence, they should generally use everyday language, a somewhat limited simple vocabulary, to sketch, ponder, and challenge the poet's world.

Acknowledgments:

Mad Thanks to my fellow poets, writers, friends, and teachers; Melanie Tague, Steve Minnich, Caitlin Mohney, Jeffery Allen, Jake Holley, Rob McDonald, Will Silverman, Anthony Mucciarone, Jennifer Atkinson, Eric Pankey, Stephen Brachlow, and Vassily Aksyonov for all the craft conversations, critiques, feedback, encouragement, and support.

Also, so much Thanks goes to Jayme Reaves, Matthew Powell, Nick Sales, Mike Baker, Sarah Amick, Cora Mabry, Gracie Kirkpatrick, and my parents for all the support and encouragement over the years.

And of course, Thank You to the many Editors and Readers who have chosen to publish my poems in their journals.

J.F. Merifield, has a Poetry M.F.A. from George Mason University, was Short Listed and published by BPM Voices' National Poetry Month Contest 2023, and has other poems published by *Wild Roof Journal, High Shelf Press, Sheepshead Review, Cathexis Northwest Press, La Picciolette Barca, Neuro Logical, Verse, Rust & Moth,* among others.

www.ingramcontent.com/pod-product-compliance
Lightning Source LLC
Chambersburg PA
CBHW030058170426
43197CB00010B/1584